as good a woman as ever broke bread

as good a woman as ever broke bread

Alex McInnis

PUNCHER & WATTMANN

First published in 2023
Published by Puncher & Wattmann
PO Box 279
Waratah NSW 2298

info@puncherandwattmann.com

NATIONAL
LIBRARY
OF AUSTRALIA

A catologue record for this book is available from The National Library of Australia.

ISBN   9781922571458

Cover design by Morgan Arnett, Alex McInnis and Emmanuel Monteiro

Printed by Lightning Source International

for Elizabeth
and
for mum

Here is a ship, an ocean.
Here is a figure, her story a few words in the blue void.

— Rick Barot

Agnes Banks, 2021

Root-nest, stone-egg.

Mum reaches into the tangled root ball of one of the fallen casuarinas and plucks out a smooth river stone. We both hope it's been there long enough to connect us to the right moment in time. The dirt and water keep flowing on and on and we flounder as we realise the old adage — that you can't visit the same river twice. But Mum says maybe this stone has been held under the changing water long enough.

Strong enough to hold a man

          down while
     his pockets are rifled;

        The Black Girl, An Old Thief.

            Strong enough to
                 bite wrist
                 blacken eye
                 cut head
                 tear shirt

                    unbutton his small clothes

                        by force!

Anne Grace's defence: I never clapped eyes on him til he took us prisoner.
Elizabeth Mandeville's defence: the same

Sentence: 7 years of transportation.

When where how & after what
manner the deceased Elizabeth Mandeville
came to her death.

The kind man who helps us find reel 6021 lets us know that these pages
are uploaded on ancestry.com, seemingly apologetic that we've made
the effort to come all the way out here. I fumble along, trying to explain
that I know there are scans online and that today we'll just be seeing a
microfilm, but I wanted to get one step closer to the real thing.

Mum and I unwind the reel of microfilm, slide it under the glass and
secure both ends. We scroll slowly at first on our way to page 435,
admiring the curling letters, wondering at what's truth or lie. So many
women who came to their deaths accidentally & by misfortune & not
otherwise. I think of my great-grandma who died chopping a pumpkin, a
knife to the belly, and how Mum always said a country woman would've
known how to chop a pumpkin.

We find our page and Mum says this guy's handwriting is shit.

On the first page is a list of names.

Patrick, James, Richard, William, George, Joseph, Andrew — all good &
lawful men of the town & County aforesaid.

All men! Mum says.

I point to the splodges next to their names.

Those are their thumb prints!

Mum's reaction is immediate and visceral —

ew!

— as if their grubby thumbs had ruptured time to poke her in the eye.

We know the story by heart — we've both read the typed transcript of the inquest into our ancestor's death online — but we have an unspoken pact to read out loud in unison, to stubbornly decipher each handwritten word, a stuttered and drawled incantation.

she

    could   ob   tain

litt le   or   no   nou   rish   ment

      ma   ny   days

&
so

           fi nal   ly

                 died

    from   want

               sick   ness

                                                    &

                   in tox i ca tion.

I invite my friends Jake and Tom to my house for the first time. Mum is chopping watermelon in the kitchen, wearing a sarong, her bare shoulders summer-brown.

Jake laughs out loud as he enters the kitchen.

I didn't know your mum was an abo!

Mum laughs along, I'm not sure if she's heard — she looks back and forth between Jake and I, her expression telling me she's missed something but doesn't want to be rude. She offers us watermelon.

Mum is a pro at playing spot the

difference,

to the point where everything

bleeds.

She's been looking for family in other
 people's faces all her life; looking for hints
of the past in her own.

I'm in the new library, at the benches by the big windows, watching the rain come down hard. It's the second time New South Wales has flooded like this in just over a year. The first was when the rains put out the fires that had burned for three months, the ash ran into the rivers and the fish went belly up. I'm catching up on uni readings about Sydney waterways while the mullet spawn and leap down Goolyari (The Cooks); reading about Marrickville floods, how the Gumbramorra swamp won't dry up and leave us in peace. There are sketches of flooded Marrickville paddocks, 'land for sale' signs poking cheekily out of the water. Black and white photos of men waist deep in flood water on a factory floor down on Carrington road, old maps with a now buried creek inked in. I open too many tabs, and wend my way to Grace Karsken's newest book, *People of The River*. She's written of Elizabeth's death in other books, and I wonder if she's found out anything more of her life.

crtl+f "mandeville"

Renting farms could be a punishing and precarious living for new and under-capitalised tenants. Landlords were sticklers for getting their payments and appeared to have wielded much power over tenants and their crops. Tenant farmers Stephen Wain and Elizabeth Mandeville rented a small farm around Agnes Banks; they had two small children, and a third about to be born. In 1821, their landlords refused to allow them to harvest their wheat. The delay would have terrible consequences for this poor tenant family.

It's the first time I've read that name — Agnes Banks. I find it on Google Maps, zoom in, zoom out, stare out the window. I think of Warragamba Dam the last time I saw it two years ago — as low as the millennium droughts, migrant labourers' graffiti exposed — now ready to overflow. I scroll Facebook. Stop. A post from the ABC tells me the Nepean has overflowed, Agnes Banks is on the evacuation list.

As we drive down the M2 and close the distance between our bodies and Agnes Banks, Mum says if she met her great-grandchildren's great-grandchildren she'd open her arms wide and say: my babies!

Thornleigh, 1999

The floors have never been this clean. I've never known air to hold it's own breath like this. I sit at the top of the stairs with the front door in sight, every particle of the house tensing itself into stillness with me.

I'm seven and I don't know what it means for a grown mother to meet her own mother. I know there was a letter and Mum cried and it was lucky her best friend who just happened to also be adopted was staying with us at the time. I know I broke the star off the end of my wand and glued it to a piece of paper to help Mum stop crying (and now I can't use it to help Dad's hair grow back).

The knock finally comes and I'm down the stairs at Mum's elbow in a flash, staring up at the new/old face that is just like hers and hardly any wrinklier. Then I have a new, life-like baby doll in my arms, Mum's new/old mum made the clothes herself and none of us should still feel a hole in our hearts.

Surry Hills, 1821

I have the honour to enclose to Your Excellency the Inquest taken
on the

wretched woman

I mentioned yesterday at the conference at Government house —

her name is Elizabeth Mandeville.

She has lived thirteen years with a settler in the district of
Castlereagh who deplores her loss as a faithful partner & the mother
of two small children.

I have the honour to remain,

Sir,

Your obedient servant

ES Hall Coroner

Evidence taken at the house of Andrew Cross.

Dr William Bland esq being sworn saith:

I saw the
        deceased
                lying
                in Cambridge St.

      She mentioned to the women
             standing
                about
                her
                    when

                                dying

          she expected to be confined
                in three weeks.

      I told them I feared
          she would

                  perish

          from
       want of
          attention.

The women

                  hesitated

        about taking her in.

    She told me
        she'd no means
            to take care of herself —
        that she'd
               taken no nourishment
             many days.
                    She thanked me.

The day I drive out to Agnes Banks, my lover tells me:
take marigolds for your ancestors.

I pluck whatever yellow flowers I can find.

When I get in the car Mum says:
chuck those out the window, they stink!

I hear my ancestors
        slap their thighs and
howl with laughter.

I'm in my first year of uni, learning about intersectionality and how to write life stories, and I want to write my grandmother's — Mum's birth-mum.

I call and arrange to visit. It's the first time I've visited alone, and I take three wrong exits on the way there, circling my way back onto the M7 each time. I turn up late with my head freshly shaved, oblivious to the shock it will give her — it's not long since her other daughter, Marie, my mother's half-sister, died from cancer. Mum and I never met her, and I try not to look too long at the photo of her in her coffin as I pass it in the hall. My grandma's bedroom door is ajar, and a dozen baby dolls with glass eyes and crocheted outfits stare at me from her bed.

We sit across from each other at her small table by the window and I hit record on my phone. I try to remember to ask open questions but I don't have to ask much.

She holds my hand and her thumb caresses the back of my thumb just like Mum's does when she's upset.

I learn some new/old things — like she only ever got to see the back of
mum's head —
that's how she could verify
that yes,
mum really did come out with
hair down to her shoulders.

and
when my grandma's sister Betty went to find their mum
after forty-odd years,
The Mum just sat there patting her little dog and saying nothing,
not where she was from or
why she left.

how no one came
to pick her up from hospital.

how the house at Toongabbie
always had a spare room
and her ex husband would say:
that's in case the baby comes back isn't it?
and she would say:
NO but so what if it is?

how she had to tell everyone
that mum was
born-dead.

how her step-mum would tell her:
keep your black hands off my babies!

and how now she's entrusted to
hold the babies on their first turn
through the revolving doors
of DOCS.

how her ex-boyfriend once said:
you're doing it for the money!
and she said:
get out!

My grandma shares freely, I don't dig. And yet I leave feeling like I've crossed into sacred ground without paying my dues; like I've taken without knowing how to give.

I get top marks for my essay unpicking the intersectionality of her life — the choices she did and didn't have, the factory jobs, the care roles she took on, the confusion of being a motherless and mysterious kind of brown in the wake of White Australia. The fullness of the marks makes my chest feel hollow. I know I'd never show my grandma what I've written, I'd rather learn how to give her a hug.

I don't visit her again for years.

Dr William Bland esq being sworn saith:

About 10 o'clock last night

    I

       received intelligence that she was

   dead

      &

    that the child was living

      &

     was requested to go up

       &

      see her immediately.

  I went

    &

    found her in the house where

       she is now lying

        quite dead

    I performed

   an operation on the deceased

&

ascertained

  the child was also

     dead.

REMEMORY | an uncanny collision or bumping into things in potent places, as spatial-temporal rupturing and ungrounded seething, waiting for recognition, knowing and reckoning for what always was and always will be.

Natalie Harkin, *Archival Poetics*

Two days before I go out to visit Agnes Banks and the archives I call
an ambulance for an Aboriginal woman who's collapsed face down
outside Broadway shops.

But not before I

hesitate.

Enough people have walked past her for a thin trail of vomit to cross
the busy footpath. The way her limbs are arranged tells me she's
lying where she fell, she hasn't been able to move. Someone has left
a pack of chips and a bottle of water at her feet. Nourishment. The
woman on the other end of the line tells me not to give her anything,
it could make her worse. Just make sure her airways are clear. I
remind myself that the echo between the document that haunts me
and the treatment of the woman lying next to me is not uncanny,
not synchronicity — it's a centuries-long, commonplace occurrence,
this blind eye towards black women's pain. I think I know better
than to flatten and conflate, to pick a thread of this woman's pain to
weave into my own basket of stories. I want to mourn/rage just for
her. I want the ambulance to get here. And yet when she manages
to lift her head a little to look me in the eyes and tries to speak, time
collapses. As she's wheeled into the ambulance the paramedic asks if
I know how long she was lying there. I point at the vomit that's crept
across the concrete as an estimate, but I want to tell him it's been 200
years.

a family story leaks out
on the wrong side of the tree,
    where we weren't looking.

                    dad's birth-mum's sister says
                    her Nanna Elsie told her:
                shhhh, I was born at La Perouse,
                but that's our little secret.

    that's why Uncle Keith
                used to get his
    knees-scrubbed-bloody —
                    skin is darkest where it
        bends and protects.

                        Aunty Lindy sends a photo.
                        I zoom in on Nanna Elsie's
                browner-than-Irish hand,
                move my face close to the screen
                        to peek under her hat
            at her jet-black hair, her high cheekbones —
    my whole body jolts as my eyes meet hers,
            my own dissecting gaze backfiring to slice me,
                            I slam my laptop closed.

now when I visit La Perouse
                I picture Nanna Elsie's mums —
            the one who raised her and the one with empty arms,
                and I don't know fact from figment —
                    birth certificate from bloodied-knees.

I practice letting my body
        be an open question —
                porous to possibility
    and doubt,
        the only way I know how
to
    honour the whispers
                that come down the line.

                now there's another old woman who
                claps me round the ear when
                        I leave
                    her out.

We're playing Pocahontas and Courtney is explaining that she gets first choice, Emma gets second and I'm last — because she has blonde hair and blue eyes, I'm brown and brown, and Emma is somewhere in the middle.

She says I have to be John Smith and she gets to be Pocahontas. I tell her she's not making sense, Pocahontas is brown and brown and John Smith is blonde and blue. I want to be Pocahontas.

But it's not about matching, it's about who gets to choose. I leave the game and nestle by the bookshelf with the hippo story that I know by heart.

Later I ask Mum about what Courtney said, and she tells me she always thought Courtney's mum was a bit of a weirdo.

It's a tiny moment, and I experience very few like it. Yet for years I use the yellow and blue textas to draw my hair and eyes. I refuse to draw my nose or ears, nothing should stick out. Especially not tummy or bum.

I use the black texta for Mum's hair — even though she tells me her hair is just very-very dark brown — and remind her that her surname is different to mine.

Revesby, 1999

come by here, my lord

kum bay aa

My cousin Jessie and I are lying on the trampoline, avoiding the
corner where the black canvas has come away from the springs
and the overgrown grass pokes through. She doesn't know where
she heard the song but she says if we sing it, it will help us to truly
connect to Animals. We've spent a long time discussing which is the
better power: to transform into any Animal, or to talk to them? And
more importantly, who gets to have which power?

Now I'm a tree and you're a possum sleeping in my branches. Trees
and possums can talk to each other.

You're a princess and I'm your loyal tiger. I'll bring you food when
you're sick (now pretend this leaf is food) and fight off any man who
wants to hump you.

Now we are both warlocks (women can be warlocks too) and these
sticks are our staffs, with purple glowing orbs on top. We can both
have any power we want.

now we are girls and we
bounce for hours
in circles on the trampoline,
shrouded in the smell of
cat piss
pot smoke
bulgogi made the best way
(tenderised in coca cola)
yelling

kum   bay   aa

ma   lord

kum   bay   aaa

43

into the sky as it gets lighter then darker. Jessie says we are circling a campfire, our tigers are in the tree keeping watch.

I like this much better than playing crack the egg, that always makes me cry.

When it's Jessie's turn to stay at my house, she writes me a poem that goes:

I love my cousin Alex so

I just want you to Know

You are just like an Angel

With your Glow

I keep it in a special tin inside the cubby house down the back.

We stand on the cubby house verandah and peg seed pods at our brothers, as they advance beneath the bushes.

When we grow up Jessie says:

You made me cry that time you said
we weren't really cousins, and do you remember how you used to say
my face is a circle cos I'm asian and yours is an oval cos
you're white?

Mum's new/old mum knows how
to snap a budgie's neck
when necessary.

Mum says she couldn't do it,
she wouldn't have the
heart.

I'm even more confused than the first time I saw
Mum cry
with joy.

London, 1783

To the Lords spiritual and Temporal, and the Commons of the
Parliament of Great Britain.

Our simple testimony is not much:

We are those who were considered as slaves.

We are of those whose

minds and bodies
are bartered from
hand to hand

on the coast of Africa as
the ordinary commo-dities of
trade.

By the horrors of that trade were we first
torn
away
from all the tender connexions
that were naturally dear to our
hearts.

When a vessel arrived to conduct us away
to the ship,
there was nothing to be heard but
rattling of chains,
smacking of whips, and
the groans and
cries of
our fellow men.

All our help was
cries and
tears and

these could not avail.

Nothing but ignorance
& the dreams of a
        viciated imagination

arising from the general countenance given to the

evil practice of wicked men,

to strengthen their hands in wickedness,
could ever make any person think that the

stealing,
kidnapping,
enslaving,
persecuting or
killing a black
man,

is in any way & manner less
criminal,
        than the same evil treatment
of
        any other man of
another complexion.

Noah was of an olive black in colour

&

if there were no buyers,
there would be
no sellers.

May the God of heaven inspire your

                                            hearts with

    peculiar benevolence   on that important day when

                              the question of

                     Abolition

                          is to be discussed.

    When   thousands,

                  in consequence of

                         your

                      Determination,

                      are to look for

                              Happiness or Misery!

                                  Signed,

                         The Sons of Africa

Olaudah Equiano
Ottobah Cugoano
George Mandeville
William Stevens
Joseph Almze
Boughwa Gegansmel
Jasper Goree
James Bailey
Thomas Oxford
John Adams
George Wallace
John Christopher
Thomas Jones
Thomas Carlisle
Daniel Christopher

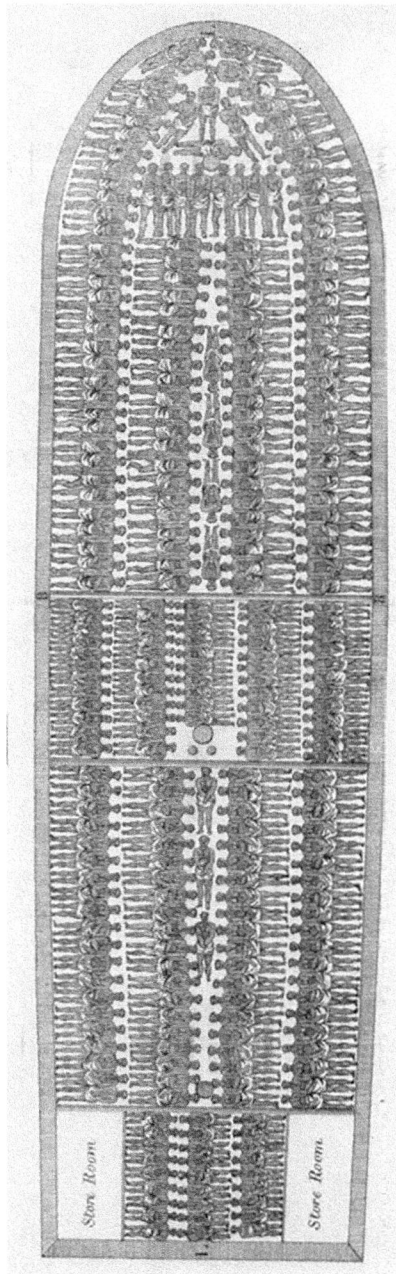

When I insert the chattel slave ship into this document, it wipes everything I've written and starts to multiply itself, one ship per page.

There are 1287 ships or

836,550 ancestors

by the time I'm able to navigate to version history, and revert to my curated arrangement.

Romarong, Sierra Leone, 1887
*the place where
men and women wept
in the storms.*

Fourteen pounds a head for
transportation
        Back To Africa,
and four months worth of
              cloth, provisions, tools.

Sixty dead before the ships leave Blackwall.

Fourteen bodies slid
              overboard
to meet gilled grandparents
in Atlantic depths.

Three hundred and eighty
            Free Black Britons
at the mouth of the Sierra Leone river,
two weeks before the monsoon
               falls.

Four hundred square miles of
salt marsh bought
from King Tom.
                    A thirteen-gun salute.

A few yellow fields of rice,
stalks no more than a foot high.

No oyster shells or lime.

No town bell to
        call the people to prayer.

No houses
        as yet.

No less than a hundred letters
destroyed or lost by
        rascal captains —
through Avarice
Or
        Indifference.

One hundred and twenty two
                Free Black Britons

                                perished
                        by September.

Two hundred and eighty six
        surviving
                Sons and Daughters of Africa
scattered to slave depots
                        seeking

                        food and shelter.

                        One future-ancestor
                        balls her fists,
                        rubs her eyes,
                leans her head against
                        her mother's chest,
                        boards a ship —
                        not her first or last.

Mum and I are sitting on the edge of the ocean pool at Freshwater, just two headlands south of Dee Why — where she learnt how to swim, and how to float face down to scare the locals; where she's asked to have her ashes scattered when it's time.

Mum's telling me that at the hairdressers that week she got asked the question she never knows how to answer: where she's from, why she's brown. She tells me she tries a different approach each time, adjusting the dose of information, the order she lets it out — testing to see which arrangement lets her slip past the awkwardness of over-sharing while satisfying the questioner.

Sometimes there's camaraderie in the question — a bid for connection: are you from where I'm from? The Filipino nurses at work tell her she looks like their most beloved pop star. When she cares for the elderly Maltese patients, she bites her tongue so not to say:

Do you know Karmnu? Tell him his baby's not dead!

Sometimes she slips, asks after his surname. They say all the Sultanas are kin.

More often, the people asking have never questioned how their own two feet got to being planted so firmly on this ground. Like the elderly white patients, whose faces shift from suspicion to open relief when they hear her Australian accent. Or Karen van Oosten from highschool, who called Mum a wog. Her friends could call her Marcia Hines with affection but Karen was a bitch, her mouth made wog a dirty word. Mum loves telling us how she came up with the best comeback (but only after van Oosten had walked away).

Mum's big bottom lip sticks out more than usual. She pulls one knee closer to her chest and her brows lower behind her sunnies as she looks out at the horizon.

She says:

I wish I could say:

My people:

But instead the ground
falls out from beneath her feet

Homebush, 2000

Mum is screaming:

        run Cathy

            run!

go   go   go   go —

        yes!

          yes!

            yes!

                  yes!

I am the voices of 80,000 people
      floating into the sky.

        My brother is crying,
hands over ears, eyes wide.

      Mum is saying:
      remember this.

wretch:
one driven out of or away from her native country; a banished person; an
exile.

On the river, people came and went like tidal flows, they bought up and sold out, little farms were partitioned off everywhere, more families and workers moved in, coupled and had babies, more huts and tents and pens sprang up, and monstrous floods washed everything away... They made everything they needed from bark, timber and hide, ground their corn for hominy, hunted, fished and foraged in the forests and swamps, cut notches in trees when they wanted to climb them, and paddled bark canoes up and down the river. Many preferred 'skins and leather' to cloth. They used fire for cooking, warmth and sociability, to burn off after harvest, to keep the forest open and to ward off darkness and devils... And whatever ancient dreams materialised in this wondrous land, settlers knew that they were not the first-comers. Everywhere they went, they encountered, not untouched wilderness, but homelands, occupied, known and tended by Aboriginal people. According to the vision for New South Wales, farming would transform and redeem land, convicts and Aboriginal people alike. But in learning to live on the river, it was the settlers' ways of life that became more like those of the people they were dispossessing.

Grace Karskens, *People of the River*

For while civil society continued in a rude state, even among the establishers of kingdoms, when they became powerful and proud, and they wanted to enlarge their territories, they drove and expelled others from their peaceable habitations, who were not so powerful as themselves. This made those who were robbed of their substance, and drove from the place of their abode, make their escape to such as could and would help them; but when such a relief could not be found, they were obliged to submit to the yoke of their oppressors, who, in many cases, would not yield them any protection upon any terms.

Ottobah Cugoano,
*Thoughts And Sentiments On The Evils of Slavery;
In an Answer to the Advocates for Slavery and Oppression*

Stephen Wain landholder & settler having been sworn saith:

she took a sample of my wheat,

    she took
        no money for I was possessed of none.

                or else she would

(here the witness wept bitterly)

she was ordinarily very sober,

as good a woman as ever
    broke bread

        at home.

I have seen her.

    as far as I have heard

      she had

            nowhere to go

(here the witness wept as he had also done most of the time)

A gull.

Water slapping sandstone.

A chain clanging somewhere.

The thrum of stretched iron,
the trains passing through the sky.

No amplified didgeridoo; no tourists.

No sparkling coins in hats,
no men in suspended animation.

Salt stench makes
you think
of oysters slicing palms.

All that quiet makes
you think
      you should
           listen harder.

Mum and I pull up in a car park just next to the bridge, where a small sandy peninsula reaches out into the Nepean river, against the current.

As soon as we get out of the car we can see what the flood has done.

The bushfire danger sign has been knocked over by high flood water, most of the casuarinas are lying down, and the riverbed has been swept up and piled high. Coarse, sandy dunes crest and dip, flowing over fallen trunks, and a layer of smooth mud has dried and cracked in the troughs. Some of the casuarinas have snapped halfway up the trunk; others have been upended, their roots grasping at air, clutching and scattering river stones. A few are left standing, and we point to the debris strung high — imagine the water rushing strong above our heads, how we'd be swept along.

I'm not sure what I'm meant to feel or do now that I'm here, or which kind of trees we are:

1. Cut off from the ground at the knees
2. Torn out at the roots
3. Standing tall with our roots reaching deep, weeds adorning our collarbones

We weave among the fallen forest, parting and returning to each other with a stone or a dried flake of mud, pointing at bird and dog tracks. Mum directs me to take a photo of a water weed splaying its blades in a near-perfect circle, with the sun reflected in its middle. Another of small green shoots swaying just above the water's surface.

We watch the river and wonder aloud how different it would have looked, and if she ever planted her feet right here and faced this way.

Mary Beauchamp (née Wain)

Elizabeth Mandeville was born in 1785 in St Giles in the Fields, London, and was one of the early women of the African diaspora to live in Sydney.

Very little is known of the details of Elizabeth's life, and what we do know was written down by others.

We know that she was the daughter of a member of the Sons of Africa — a group of former slaves fighting for abolition in London — and that her family were among the few survivors to return to London from the doomed colony of 'Free Black Britons' in Sierra Leone.

In her early twenties, Elizabeth was convicted of theft and transported to Sydney, arriving on the 26th of January 1809. She lived with her common law husband, Stephen Wain, on a bend of the Nepean River near Castlereagh with their two children, William and Mary.

The inquest into Elizabeth's death states that she passed away while heavily pregnant in 1821, after having travelled to The Rocks with neighbours to sell a sample of wheat; been robbed of her earnings and not able to find her neighbours to return home; and spending a number of days in the streets of The Rocks without access to food, water or medical care.

This collection draws on archival documents and the research of others, as well as my own life and family tree — as a descendant of Elizabeth, and as the daughter of multiple generations of adoption, separation, secrecy and reunion on both sides of the family.

The process of research and writing has been as much about deepening intimacy with the gaps in story as it has been about threading together the fragments. Since childhood I've returned to the few moments of Elizabeth's life available to me with a deepening sense of curiosity and love — all of my questions opening up to more questions, and the gaps becoming a fertile home for imagination, curiosity, disorientation and deep knowing to co-exist.

I imagine that Elizabeth would speak in chorus with Jeanine Leane's archival women, reminding us when reading:

> When you read about me on record,
> don't let 'em tell you they knew me.
> Remember how you knew me — remember what
> I remembered with you
> when you read I was wanton, wild, despicable.

Cugoano, O. (1787). Thoughts and sentiments on the evil and wicked traffic of the slavery: And commerce of the human species, humbly submitted to the inhabitants of Great-Britain, by Ottobah Cugoano. London, 1787

Equiano, O. (1793). The interesting narrative of the life of Olaudah Equiano: or, Gustavus Vassa, the African.
Karskens, G 2020, People of the river : lost worlds of early Australia , Allen & Unwin, Crows Nest, NSW.

Leane, J 2018, Walk back over , Corditebooks, Calton South, Victoria.

Hanley, R 2018, Beyond Slavery and Abolition: Black British Writing, c.1770–1830

Harkin, N 2019, Archival-poetics , Vagabond Press, Sydney, New South Wales.

Hoare, P. (1820) Memoirs of Granville Sharp, Esq [electronic resource] : composed from his own manuscripts, and other authentic documents in the possession of his family and of the African Institution / by Prince Hoare : with observations of Mr. Sharp's biblical criticisms, by the Right Rev. the Lord Bishop of St. David's ... London: Printed for H. Colburn.

Pybus, C 2006, Black founders : the unknown story of Australia's first black settlers , UNSW Press, Sydney.

NSW State Archives and Records, 1821 Jan 13 Inquest on body of taken in Cambridge Street, Sydney (Reel 6021; 4/1819 pp.435-40)

Old Bailey Proceedings Online, April 1808, trial of ANN GRACE ELIZABETH MANDEVILLE (t18080406-50).

www.ingramcontent.com/pod-product-compliance
Lightning Source LLC
Chambersburg PA
CBHW030854090426
42737CB00009B/1230